The Inquisition
(The Voice of Nevada Poets)

Edited by Ferris E. Jones

Copyright
by Ferris E. Jones
All Rights Reserved

ISBN: 978-0-6151-9253-6
ID:2014597
www.LuLu.com

This book is dedicated to the wonderful people who call Northern Nevada home.

Table of Contents

Mary Nevada Lambert..........................Trying to Paint the Desert
                                            His Final Days
                                            The White Flags of Babyland
Trever Crow .... Yellow Journalism
                                            Untitled # 1
                                            Nightmare
                                            Untitled # 2
                                            Childhood Memories at Random
                                            A Book Review
                                            Anasazi Lines
Mary Santomauro......................................Bohemian Blue
                                            Francis Scott Key
                                            Aztec
                                            The Boy and the Butterfly
                                            The Pirate
                                            Just for Me
                                            Tree Waltzer
                                            That House
                                             For Don
                                            A Gift Sublime
Barry DeMars… ....The Devil's Playground
                                            Angel's Wings
                                            Cowboy's Justice
                                            Elusive Red Gold
                                            My Greatest Christmas Memory
J.D. Littlewolf.......................................The Bridge to Life
                                            The Morning Light
                                            In a Meadow
                                            Alone
                                            My Life Changed
Peter J. Metz................................ .Heroes of "Old"
Joshua German.................. ....Hangin with Death
Angelita Froid...................... ....…..Double Delight
Leigh McGuire............................. .... …..Any Good News
                                            Shopping for the Apocalypse
Rikku.. . .Delusion Truth
Sarah Tomlinson............................ ... Kombucha Dowry
Catherine Dotta............................ .... .Song of Spring
                                            Lonesome Rose
Ashley Rubin.............................…....... .The Watchful Eye
                                            Moments to Remember

Arthur Winfield Knight............................Hoppy's Favorite
                                                 The High Plains
Kit Knight..Mildred, 1943 executed by Hitler
                                                 The Bruises of Loss
Penny McCracken...................................Just One Man
                                                 The Mermaid Awaits
Ferris E. Jones.......................................The Beats #12
                                                 Religions Everywhere
                                                 In the Midst of Things
                                                 Children's
                                                  Equal
                                                  Thought
                                                  The Club
Debra A Bobelak....................................Silent Rain
Cheryl L. Poole................................... …Autumn
Mary Meckler....................................... ...Desert Dirt
                                                 A Happening
Greg F. Cawdrey............................ ....Heat Carved
                                                 Regret
Chris Nolan..Prayer for a Friend
Diannea Hickey......................................The Magic of Music
Annalisa Stark.......................................A Swingset
Harold Roy Miller....................................Virginia City is Still Alive and Well

Trying to Paint the Desert

I took some canvas, brushes and paint.
And went into the desert to recapture what I saw.
I looked at the colors, some dark and some faint,
And found I could only look about me with awe.

This is pure desolation to a stranger of the desert,
So many feel "This is the God Forsaken Land."
It's a sight of wonderment to one who loves the desert,
You and its creator view its wonders hand in hand.

The silence, the vastness, the clear and brilliant light.
The deepening of the colors with the coming of the night,
I looked about me to decide on a theme,
Before I knew it, I was as though in a dream.

Every minute I watched the colors change and come alive.
One whole range of mountains changed as if a giant stride.
I could see no living creature, yet nature was at play.
I reluctantly folded my easel and turned and walked away.

His Final Days

If your town is like mine, there's a section called "Old Man's Row."
If you are like me, it is one of the saddest sights you know.
These poor old men who live with memories all day long.
Memories of homes, filled with loved ones, long since gone.
Clothes once so immaculate, now so unclean.
Lost in reverie, enveloped in a dream.
I sorrow for these empty men, with all meaning gone from life.
Who's lonesomeness started with the passing of an aged wife.
Too old to find new interests, too old to start again.
Who have often outlived the few men they could call a friend.
My heart goes out to men who live their final days like this.
This is an ending to life, I pray the men I love will miss.

The White Flags of Babyland

Once again babies wash must be done.
I admire it's snowy whiteness in the sun.
I watch the breeze unfurl the little white flag.
And reach for another one in the bag,

Flags are flown for nobility throughout the world,
Their arrival is announced when their flag is unfurled.
Although not intricate of design, or of many hue,
The "Little King" of this household has one too.

His arrival was announced to all within sight,
By immediately unfurling his flag of white.
The "White Flag of Babyland" which flies today,
Announces "His Majesty" has come to stay.

Yellow Journalism

front page newspaper
foreign enemy doppelganger
a pic of Saddam in a hole
hair stylist went overboard on his hair

did that make you feel tuff and proud?
you missed it as it passed – a snow cloud
a funny cartoon clown
WMD's in his pocket as he walks around

a con on the public
its time the people con the government
like Fidel posing misfits as refugees
handing out keys for opportunities

i flipped the war coin till it landed on tails
in the desert, be weary of sweet smells
and don't look up in the city
did i forget to mention his hanging? pity

pity, that you bought it – you're worse than a snitch
that clip was shakier than the blair witch
nonsense bet…you gullible fool
i bet your convictions are as blurry as that video

Untitled # 1

we all flake the same color skin
be you black, white, or reptilian
the snake molts & the lava's molten
the star gazes &
the human passes thru phases
with our pasts drawing mazes

serious to smart to funny to peculiar
most puzzle pieces are shaped similar
I live in the place of shark gods in desert lands
where hands are mastered by invisible bands
a black man with an albino chromosome
a white man with civil rights megaphone

catch the hurst
let he who is without cast the first
flashes of images
lashes of magic twigs

i freed my shadow & waved good-bye to my reflection
embraced my past life as a horse-less Indian
i didn't think i'd be able to write again
but a voice prompted me by sayin'
"come on boy – don't stop believin
cuzz dreamin' is what separates you from the heathen"

nightmare

i met a girl and tried to sketch her
her name was universe – she was spectacular
my hand got pulled into the pad of paper
i kept drawing & got sucked in even further
got lost like staring at the art of Escher
i reached up and tried to grab an answer
but the canvas stretched & tightened like prison walls of a dungeon even deeper
and i started seeing PAN's characters walking around everywhere
scared, i felt like a leper
in the presence of PAN's violent laughter
he kept blinding my eyes with watercolor
the longer i was in this world i realized there were things i could alter
i felt in control like i had some kind of special power
things would change whenever i spoke or gestured
stuff would disappear then reappear
objects were replacing one another
when a single object left, universe lost a little luster
it seemed as if a copy of universe were being taken with it elsewhere
stripped of her genius layer by layer
i watched a mother give birth to a clone of herself and lay bare

Untitled # 2

i met a girl and tried to sketch her
my hand got pulled into the pad of paper
i kept drawing & got sucked in even further
got lost like staring at the art of Escher
i reached up and tried to grab an answer
but the canvas stretched & tightened like prison walls of a dungeon even deeper
and i started seeing PAN's characters walking around everywhere
he kept blinding my eyes with watercolor
until i realized i didn't need those old perceptions any more
the longer i was in this world i realized there were things i could alter
i felt in control like i had some kind of special power
things would change whenever i spoke or gestured
stuff would disappear then reappear
objects were replacing one another
when a single object left, the universe lost a little luster
it seemed as if a copy of the universe were being taken with it elsewhere
this is why mine is different than your future

Childhood Memories at Random

Throwin' rocks at bottles down by the railroad tracks
Nowhere near October but we can still be seen all day wearin' our masks
Throwin' dirt clad grenades, screamin' "wolverines!"
It's our summer scream & we're playin' make believe
Grandpas cheating at jeopardy
Great grandmas really pissin' in a pot
Neighborhood kids – nobody won but we all fought
Up to no good – all the cousins are out stealing mail
Jesus! Did you see what we made that other kid eat out the garbage pail?
Threw away all the salt in the house just to save one snail
Buildin' forts in trees or on the gound
Cover our skin in mud from a hose-soaked dirt mound
My cat named "Nobody" ran away
"Mom! (ma) go see if the twins wanna come out "n" play
Up-down, up-down, left-right, left-right, a-b, a-b, select-start
Wagons, bb guns, slip "n" slide made outa tarps
Chewin' on gum – tradin' baseball cards
Calling Mario's "fireballs" spit wads
Ninja turtle action figures livin' (insida) Lincoln Logs
Down by the creek catchin' crawdads and pollywogs
Honeysuckle nights fulla tree frogs
Childhood is sweet trouble like a principle's office
Squeeze this pen into my fist as I remember childhood bliss

A Book Review

Rhonda Byrne, why'd u name ur book <u>The Secret</u>?
that title sounds like nothing more than a marketing
gimmick

since birth i've been an amateur scientist
as a child i knew ur secret (lika) quantum physicist

ain't it common knowledge that thoughts make up reality?
u act as if it's some kinda big conspiracy
saying that the only people who ever knew about it were
the wealthy

i know without putting a name on it
i chose not to get any fame from it

Anasazi Lines

Anasazi lines
linear spines
disappearing tribes
culture collides
bodiless lifes
free from times
history divides

Bohemian Blue

Do you know you spring from Bohemia
Capped by the White Carpathians?
You grew from the middle Danube,
Volcanic spas and rock formations,
As pleasing as your edelweiss.Fescue holds your footprint
and primrose marks your path.
High meadows crib your flora
With Solomon's rival, lily-and the beautiful anemone.
The bear, wolf, lynx, and wildcat
Stalk your pumpernickel forests
As well as deer and wild boar,But the eagle,
The golden and white-tailed eagles
Rule your eye-blue skies!You are dour Bohemian,
The quick-emotioned Slovak
Knitted through the centuries
By the geniality of the Moravian.
You are a child of the Prague Infante'.
Are you also ecclesia catholica?
Or does St. Wenceslas slide from your tongue,
A mere ritual of boughs decked with holly?
What a beautiful fountain you spring from!
It bubbles with dark forest lush.
It is cast into sandstone formations,
A Miocene primordial brush!

Francis Scott Key

He stood upon the starboard deck
Gaze fixed on embattled scenes.
Sulphuric fumes attacked the nostrils,
Opened thought of dire death-dreams
And all the horrid things
Coming with inhumanities:
Brother pit against brother
Even against whole families.
His heart was torn, but no escape,
They were committed, no return.
Stomach knotted; fists clenched.
Their cause was just, this was their concern,
But it could be no other way,
The path, clear to everyone.
They must be strong against the foe,
The breath of freedom, if they won.
And as the night continued on
Cannons roared their rights demand;
Sail staffs broken, houses crushed,
Blood washed shores of this proud land.
The scene of death was all around

He could taste it in the air
And as the day crept up the sky
He saw our flag still flying there.
His heart beat strong; joy screamed inside.
This moment would soon be gone.
He had to let the whole world know
And so he penned this song,
"Oh, say, can you see by the dawn's early light,"
And his eyes filled with tears of joy
As he wrote the heart of a brave new nation,
Please, God, let none destroy!

Aztec

Billowing clouds rolled slowly back
And into hazy view
Came myriads of the long ago,
Heads plumed in peacock blue.

The temple steps rose toward the sky
Their secret still untold.
Sliding doors hid deep inside
A nation's might in gold.

Orange sun broke across the sky.
All bowed their heads, adored
The god who came to greet them,
Their spirits now restored.

I watched with awe-struck eyes
This vision from the past
And could not understand the tongue
I heard them speak at last.

The chieftain stood tall as his mount,
His cloak, gold-woven threads,
And in his hand the staff of king
Above the milling heads.

He stood atop the mountain
And looked both far and wide
His body bronzed by ageless suns
No raiment could hide.

Golden trinkets, ingot size,
Hung loosely from his neck.
And lo, the eyes that fell on me
Were kindred to Aztec.

Then I saw him move toward me
With slow deliberate pace.
Terrified, I backed away.
Waking filled dream-space.

The Boy and the Butterfly

It was slightly mauled
By something larger
Than its young and tender self
Laying helpless in the driveway.
The young boy gently picked him up,
Its imperceptible feet
Clinging to the fingers
Extended to its reach.
Two sympathetic eyes
Perceived its sadly plight
And sought to ease
Its pain…a mercy death.
Three drops of formaldehyde
Would end its suffering.
But in the morn, no stiff remains.
Instead, a butterfly in flight
Flitting mid the curtains.
So now he offers honey,
A drop of flower nectar.
Velvet night steps aside for day.
One more flower gives to it
The strength to fly away.

The Pirate

The red scarf covers his hair,
A black patch hides one eye,
And dangling from one ear,
A blue and silver ring.
He limps with a stiffened leg
And carries an ugly sword.
Hanging from one arm
A stumped hook-hand,
Blood dripping down its sides.
And fearsome as he is
I just cannot conceal
The merriment I feel
As I watch him try
To climb into the car
With stiffened leg unbending.

Just for Me

It was raining this morning…
Leftovers from the night before
When she left for work.
Her job is now a "bummer drag"
Depressing her for several weeks.
She glances out the third-story window,
Picks up the phone, kk and I hear…
"It is still raining softly.
I can see clouds over the mountains.
There is a fog, too, and the wind is blowing.
'The sun is shining and there is a rainbow,
All at the same time It's beautiful!"
The, tenderly, she adds…
"God did this just for me!"
And I had to agree!

Tree Waltzer

He waltzes on trees sixty feet high
Using a gas saber to trim pesty saplings.
Sun glistens on his blue-black hair
Cut half-way down his neck
But for the red strands kiting in the breeze.
His Indian-skin beads with droplets
Spilling iridescence on his tattooed arms.
Movements, he executes precisely.
Though safely shackled to the mast
He leaves no room for error.
Boots spike into bark
Allowing him to meticulously walk
The riggings of the cottonwood.

That House

I love that house!
Just enough room for mine.
Flake-snow outside, chillin',
Hearth inside, warmin'\
Comfy toes,
Reddened nose,
And, I suppose
Lots of good things to eat.
Nice warm bed to cuddle in,
Blankets thick-as-can-be,
Motif-sheets spillin' from curtains
Drawn against the stars.
Nights to dream
Delicious schemes
Built in that house I love!

For Don

He never gives one any more
Than that which one can bear.
And with each trial, He sends His grace
To hold us through the fare.

He wants to fashion us a joy
Of everlasting touch.
He uses trials to steele us.
Cost of this joy not much

If you compare it to the Cross
Upon which Jesus died.
Think! A God became a man
And all our tears He cried!

So when we have no more desire
To fight the wars of life
And feel the battle is not worth
All this strain and strife,

Remember, all our tribulations
That numb us with their rod
Fall like severed petals
Before the smile of God!

A Gift Sublime

A long time ago
In a very lowly town
A babe was born one night,
And Him, nearby shepherds found.
They didn't' know about His birth
Till they heard angels sing
Giving them glad tidings
Of a lone-awaited King.
The Babe was in a manger
Just as the angels told.
His bed was straw that oxen eat.
He was bundled from the cold.
Then came three kings from far away
With gold, frankincense and myrrh…
Special gifts for a newborn King.
They were guided by a brilliant star.
This babe, one day, would lay down
His life for all mankind
The greatest gift that one can give…
A perfect gift, sublime.
In this He set an example
Of how each of us should live
And all of you have followed
With what you and yours now give.

The Devil's Playground

Out there in the distance,
where the dust swirls
around.
In the heart of this desert,
known as the devil's
playground.
They stood upon the barren
land,
and swore a bitter oath.
To make it from this baking
hill,
Lest it take them both.
They trudged for miles,
in the baking sun,
towards the distant hills.
Each step a little closer,
the sand their boots it fills.
The wicked fate overtook
them,
upon the barren clay.
And there is where we found
them,
water but just a few feet
away.

And so here we buried
them,
an epitaph to the cursed
groun'.
He is in his Sunday best,
she in her wedding gown.
Out there in distance,
where the dust swirls
around.
Two more souls shall ever
wander,
among the sands of
the devil's playground.

Angel's Wings

Though our hearts are broken,
we hear as the angel sings.
As God has given another soul,
a brand new pair of wings.
A thousand candles lit for him,
there within his home.
A million more shining bright,
in the hearts that he has known.
Fly high my friend to heaven's door,
for God has called you nigh.
A poet's story you must tell,
to the Lord on high.
As farewell we say,
to you my friend.
Your work here done,
and at it's end.
But your memory,
each poet sings.
For God He's given you,
a pair of angel's wings.

Cowboy's Justice

He stood in the saddle,
and searched acrossed the land.
Looking for the outlaw,
t'was to die by his hand.
He took from him everything,
that made the cowboy's life.
He ran off all his cattle,
burned his cabin and killed his wife.
So the cowboy tracked him,
across the dusty plain.
He will follow him forever,
through dust and driving rain.
When he catches up to him,
his gun will be the law.
Revenge will be his justice,
for the destruction he saw.
None shall ever fault him,
Upon this deadly trail.
For death the only reason,
that he should ever fail.
Then there upon the street, in a dusty town.
The cowboy and the killer,
had the last showdown.
Guns ablaze in glory,
the outlaw's shot did miss.
The cowboy killed him there,
for the wife he'll never kiss.

Elusive Red Gold

Bold and daring are these,
the men of the Bering Sea.
Holding close the danger,
of life or eternity.

They bear the wind,
they bear the waves,
and the unrelenting cold.
Searching forever for,
that elusive red gold.

They stand upon,
the starboard rail,
setting all their traps.
Hoping to find,
the mother-load,
or pulling up but scraps.

They work for hours,
and fight the ice,
for to fill their hold.
Reaching deep below the waves,
for their share,
of that elusive red gold.

But remember now,
those who gave their all,
till death took a hold
They gave you their share,
you have it there,
that damned elusive red gold.

Fish on young man,
through the biting cold.
May God help you in your search,
for that elusive red gold.

We shall pray for your safe return,
and that you've filled your goal,
but if the sea should take your life,
to God we commend your soul.
And may he grant your passage,
and keep you with full hold,
there upon that grand old boat,
the 'ELUSIVE RED GOLD'

My Greatest Christmas Memory

As I stand here by the window,
and the snow begins to fall.
I remember each Christmas,
loving them all.
For it wasn't the presents,
all wrapped with bows.
Nor the ties or the socks,
with finger like toes.
But the family love,
that's most dear to me.
As I look deep down,
in my Christmas memory.
The cheery little faces,
of our children there.
Of puppies and kittens,
with soft down hair.
Of grandma's cooking,
passed down to mom.
To the snowman out front,
built by uncle Tom.
Yes, my Christmas memories,
are all I have left now,
but remember them I do,
but by far My Greatest
Memory,
Will always be you.

The Bridge to Life

I knew one day I would find a place
A place where all fears would fade away.
I spent my entire life trying to hide
Trying clever ways, I thought, to conceal
Afraid to let anyone see the real me.
I knew one day I would find a place
A place to build a bridge to You.
I was looking for a road or a path
A narrow road to love, to strength
A path to understanding.
I knew one day I would find a place
A place of sparkling waters.
There has been so much missing in my life
I wanted to let the love enter in
I no longer wanted to be alone.
Did I let it just happen?
Or, did someone bring me here?
To this place of peace and contentment
The place to build a bridge to You.
Never to go alone again, or, in fear.
I have found the place I looked for
The place to let my feelings free.
A place to let God enter in
With His love, His strength
And, His understanding.

The Morning Light

The morning sun shone bright in his face
As the little man stood with his head held high
His torn and tattered clothes hung loosely on his thin frame
He stood alone clutching a small paper bag
Gazing toward the sky.

Then I saw the tears in his eyes
The pain and suffering in his face
Some looked down on him and scurried away
A tear came to my eyes – they couldn't see his face
Nor the tears as he stood alone gazing toward the sky.

As I approached the little man
He called to me – "Come closer please
Enjoy the morning light with me.
I am told of green grass and the trees
I feel the morning sun upon my face
But, tell me what you see."

As I shared the beauty all around little man smiled
The tears faded away
And he said to me,
"Thank you for sharing the beauty you see
For I am blind
But, in my heart I see."

In a Meadow

High above a mountain ridge
The Golden Eagle soars.
His screech is heard
In the meadow far below.
He circles the grassland
Searching for his score.
Up and down he glides with ease
His keen eye watching
For movement on the ground.
Hunger drives him on and on
Diving and circling the meadow below.
The he sees a rabbit and a doe.
With precision as a diamond cutter
He circles his prey with extended claws
And dives to capture the rabbit unaware.
His screech is heard throughout the valley
As he takes to flight
With prey in tow.

Alone

I miss the time of being alone
Alone
To dream.
Alone
To wander.
To run through field in my mind
To scream if need be.
Sitting by the fireplace
The blaze glowing
So bright and warm.
Letting my mind escape
Floating to the clouds
Bouncing from star to star
To visit the moon if I so desire.
To sit alone
With my own special dreams.
All the special moments
Only found
 In being
 Alone.

My Life Changed

The day we met my life changed.
Years of loneliness and being alone
Nights of TV dinners and sleeping alone.
The hours and the days seemed to fly by
The day we met when my life changed.

Long walks on the beach
Laying by the fire on cold winter nights
Watching the sun set then gazing at the moon.
Holding you close, and being held close
I thank God for the day we met.

A home and someone to come home to
Curling up with a good book
Glancing over at you the same time you glance at me.
We took two lonely lives and made one
A life of happiness, a fulfilled world of love.

The day we met my life changed.
Caring, sharing, wanting and needing
Having all hopes and dreams come true.
The day we met you changed my life
And I thank God for you.

Heroes of "Old"

There are so many heroes; we see them everyday,
But seldom recognize them, they are mostly shades of gray.
The woman in her threadbare coat, her figure stooped and bent, walks slowly among the sidewalk, deciding on food, or rent.

The old man sitting on the bus, tired, and full of fears,
Asks God, humbly, for the strength, to grind out two more years.
A homeless man, waits for food, hoping no one sees him shiver,
Then, quietly sits in a corner, asking blessings for the giver.

A man of sixty-three, plays with two boys, four, and ten,
His daughter had brought them a year ago, and had not returned since then.
An old woman sits in a wooden chair, huddled by the heater,
She can barely remember the face of the man, who savagely had beat her.

In a county ward, there lays a man, with a face of chiseled stone,

He waits without complaining, to die there, all alone.
A veteran, in a wheelchair, slowly sips his warm, flat beer,
And remembers, that when duty called, he was first to volunteer.

These are the faceless heroes, that surround us every day,
And we all without a conscious thought, almost always turn away.
Occasionally we risk a glance, and see what they've become,
And give nary a thought, to the battles fought, by heroes, every one.

Hangin with Death

Ever felt death looking you over? Looking around, Taking
someone you love? The piercing eyes of someone who is
not there? The touch, the smile, the arrogance your self put
on display?
Have you ever enjoyed it? Looked back,
smiled. Invited him over? Straight missed his
company? Ever got jealous? Wonder why
you were left out…………….reminded?
It's a thing of understanding, it's a thing of
respect. Ya I get a little jealous sometimes.
I miss that guy sometimes. I've seen him sooo
many times. I knew he was there. I've looked
him in the eyes. He let me go. I fell asleep in
his arms. He let me go.
There ain't nothing like livin. After you've been
hangin with death. Things smell better. They
taste better.
There is the real artist. How else could we
appreciate what we do have, until we dangle
on the edge? How else could we walk the line? It's our pain
that refines us, defines us.
Turns us into who we really are. Therefore
at least for me death will have a few props.

Double Delight

Watch double delight Rose grow
and you have watched a woman grow.
As a dainty bud to a full bloom of beauty, so does she.
Shades of red shows her fire,
Pink, her playfulness,
Yellow, her peace,
White, her curiosity.
With all the beauty of a rose, one can also feel her wrath.
A prick reminds you treat her right.
The fragrance of double delight intoxicates you.
Like her sensual self.
After the rose dries, its petals remind you of its beauty.
Only to stay with you in joyful memory.

Any Good News

What do I need to do today?
Is there any good news in the world today?
Is there any ice on the highway today?
Has the price of gas gone up today?

Was I impolite to you yesterday?
Did I watch too much C-Span yesterday?
What did I neglect yesterday
that was still a day away?

And, oh, my dear sweet dying lord,
what about tomorrow?

Shopping for the Apocalypse

Bottles of water, gallons of gas, blankets,
dried beans, rice. Use cash, don't spend it all
in one place, two, or three. Unload supplies
quietly into the basement, maybe at night.

Mail-order a hand-cranked radio, solar lamps, seeds.
Buy Q-tips, kerosene, candles. Sort through books,
Downloadable music, reruns of "X-Files" on DVD.
What's important?

Have friends bring you antibiotics from Tijuana.
Buy vitamins, batteries, tuna, salt, barley.
Sweep the chimney. Get new shoes.
Get that cavity filled.

Stock up on bourbon and bullets.
Acquire trade goods –
Cigarettes, wine, marijuana.
Watch the news, read the blogs,
find time for target practice.

Keep cash on hand. Don't forget
dog food. Think about God.

Hurry.

Delusion Truth

A happy family fits the perfect picture.
When the family laughs and are generous to one another;
it seems to warm your soul.
Under those laughter lies a deep secret paradox.
The mother once inside her house undress her true colors.
She dominates her husband and child, controlling their faith
by sucking their ambition into destruct power.
The father sulks and drowns into his own sorrow, wishing
He could go back to his past to fix the mistakes he made.
He does not try to be strong for his daughter.
The only child learns to grow on her own as she gets older.
Without her mother's love and her father's strength.
She wonders if her existence is for the other members of
the family cruel entertainment.
As the mother, father, and their daughter go outside as a
"family".
Their behavior is all staged as an act when the curtains are
opened.
When their act is all done and the curtains closed.
Back into the family's house unveils the non-fiction
ugly side hidden from the audience.
In the end the audience are fooled by a simple act.
Tricked into the "truth" instead of "realistic".

Kombucha Dowry

the beginning of it is a name
the little girl asks
are they all like this

must I be in love
with a girl so terribly young
and beautiful

Carlos the photographer
is still younger
must I model for him

the large German women
speak in diminutives

I feel a little disembodied
I live in a desert city

the wind howls coolly outside
through the falling sun
my plants are good

my life is a happy mess
full of failure, which

canceling itself out makes
a salad of small successes
I tape it to the refrigerator
the wind howls and howls
it gladdens me
I wonder who it's scaring
who waits alone
in the middle of the day
waiting
embarrassed by some childhood memory
with their pants down
and toothpaste smeared across the mirror
there are no rules anymore

the police are ninnies
the sages are the police
only time falling
unevenly

over everything
50 years is nothing
and I am already the most important prince
with the biggest herd of yaks
licking each other

what is your dowry
how can I please your father
so that you too will know
this wind
this gorgeous howling wind

Song of Spring

Softly seeking spring has come alive.
Moonlit blossoms touch the velvet sky.
Crescent gardens blushing pink imply.
Rustic splendor to my aspiring eye.

Springtime casts a picture of enchantment there.
Among sweet gathered petals etched separately divine.
Rusting bows accompany this silent starlit night.
A blissful spell has sought its proper place in Spring.

Lonesome Rose

You have become a rose to me.
A cherished petal of life to me.
An innocent bloom amidst passions plea.
I vow a sacred gift to thee.
Acknowledge this and you will be,
The one to share each day with me.

The Watchful Eye

The eyes hold the most expressions
memories of joy and life hidden in the depths of the soul
Moving left to right up and down focusing on a target
Seeking out weaknesses and vulnerabilities
If looks could kill the thoughts can destroy
Thoughts and stares of cold stone only meant to discourage
Only punctilious thoughts searching for ways to manipulate dwell
Looking at the eyes one can' hide, exposing what dwells inside
Giving intimidating looks exposing false testimonies leading to confessions
The hands of the face scanning the surface for impurities
Then sending warning signs of danger and moving away
The eyes that see what is true
The eyes that hold expressions, memories, and fears
The eye is always watching like a hawk stocking its prey

Moments to Remember

Moments can bring out the best in each other
moments are meant to be shared with another
moments can make you laugh or sing with each other
Surrealistic dreams won't seem out of reach
because moments are no longer at a dreams reach
A picture is worth a thousand words
A smile can tell a thousand stories
A laugh feeds the soul with screams of joy
A hug cuddles the heart with sweet words
To receive love from another
To prove hate to each other
To feel emotion and show affection
Is not to feel or be received as cold as stone
To wipe the tears of sorrow and replace them with tears of joy
With moments happier days are upon the horizon
Through secret messages and code that show how much love and care is given
Nothing brings more joy to the heart than creating a smile
An hour can seem like a second
A second can seem like an hour
But with a love one second can be an eternity
Surprising moments unwanted moments
Loving moments hateful moments
These will always be the moments, and memories for us to remember

Hoppy's Favorite

I remember buying a quart of milk
with Hoppy's picture on it
when I moved to Citrus Heights.
It said the milk was Hoppy's favorite,
and I wondered how many kids
remembered him. It was 2002,
and he'd been dead 30 years.
I remember my mother took me
to see Hoppy in San Francisco
the year I turned 12, because
he was my favorite cowboy star.
I heard his boots hitting the floor
before I saw him, coming
down the hall at the Emporium,
his spurs jingling. I got
his autograph and a picture
of Hoppy on his horse, Topper.
I hadn't thought of Hoppy in years
until I saw him pictured
on that blue milk carton,
wearing his black hat, smiling.
It was good to see him again.

The High Plains

The light in the trees
looks like cotton candy
when we walk the dog
most mornings,
the moon still visible,
like a sliver of dried ice,
above the old courthouse.
By mid-afternoon
the light in the trees
is sepia-tinted
when we go to the bar
at Casino West.
CNN is always on.
The barmaid knows
Kit and I will be there,
The 4 o'clock people.
Often, in the winter,
the stars are ice crystals
in a frozen sky
by the time we leave.
The clouds,
shaped like saucers,
are tangerine colored.
It's a good life.

Mildred, 1943
Executed by Hitler

Her head was chopped off.
Mildred was born in Milwaukee,
met and married her husband
there, then followed him
back home. Arvid was
German. Mildred taught English
at the University of Berlin.
The couple became members
of a resistance group helping
German Jews escape. The group
began sending coded messages.
When the Nazis found
the spy ring, they arrested
the young couple, along with
135 others. The first secret
trial ended with Arvid
being hung and Mildred
ordered to serve six years.
Because she was an
American, Hitler wanted
to make an example
of her. Another
secret trial. But this time
Hitler was satisfied. Mildred
was taken to the room where

her husband had been hung
two months earlier and
a guillotine was waiting.
Mildred Harnack, the only
American woman executed
by special orders of Adolf
Hitler. That's a tribute.

The Bruises of Loss

Ann was in her 70's, retired
from a hospital job preparing
meal trays. For 30 years, on each
holiday, Ann crocheted pins
and every patient's tray
was graced with a shamrock
or a tiny green wreath
with red balls. I grew up
next door and often danced
into Ann's house. Especially
on Easter. Psanka. Ann spent
days etching fine beeswax lines
to dye Ukrainian eggs. She always
made me a special one. I was 17
when the care hit me and
didn't understand I'd carry
the bruises of loss forever. I
spent seven months in hospitals.
When my family visited me
That Easter morning my mother
Held a dazzling psanka egg, saying
"Ann brought it last night." As
years passed, I visited Ann
each time I went to see

my parents. Upon retiring,
Ann's gifts became more
Elaborate. The soft white
Crocheted basket was only
two inches across. Red ribbon
entwined the rim and perched
in the basket was a yellow
crocheted chickie with
orange feet. It's been 17 years
since she gave it to me.
Last night my mother called
saying, "Ann died." I cuddle
my basket and everything
rushes back.

Just One Man

He was just one man;
Polish born, his name Karol Woitewa.
He saw the Nazis invade his home, survived the horror,
and began as a simple priest.

Many years later, he had visited most of the world,
his strength, goodness and decency
was even part of the death of Communism.
He inspired even those with whom he could disagree
yet he could always touch their hearts, and ours.

His death left so many feeling bereft;
it will be hard to find another such as he.
And his death, and funeral,
Stopped the World.
For a brief time, millions stopped in harmony
people of all faiths mourned him –
even some with no faith at all.

For a brief, wonderful time
the world stopped
the wars stopped
the hatred stopped.

Please, can we now stop, listen, help each other?

Can we no longer hate each other
When we love and worship the same God,
Can we stop fighting, over silly differences
in HOW we worship the same God;
or by what name we call Him –
when His name just sounds different
in each of our many languages.
We are all children of the same Father'
And this gentle and simple man taught us.
Can we please stop?

How would the world look –
if we reached out to each other/
Does it take a tsunami, earthquake or hurricane
or death of a Pope
to give us such a simple, loving message?

Let us turn to –
help the homeless, feed them until they can feed themselves
empty our pockets of weapons, and fill them
with the tools to recreate civilizations.
Love one another,
As His simple message has called
down through millennia.
The death of one man
stopped the world, for so brief a time.
Let's keep it going –
All it takes is the love we poured out so recently.
He led the way, now let us follow.

The Mermaid Awaits

I see my child, walking lonely on the shore
and ache to greet her and comfort her battered spirit.
But I cannot, the rules are firm;
my child, and the children of my child
must come here, each of their own accord
and only when the time has come.

I hear her, see her, see what the relentless years have done
what gravity she bears on tired bones.
She looks now all the age that I myself, was spared.
I want to go to her, tell her
"When you join me, you once again shall be young,
be able to swim as one day we dreamed.
The Ocean, Neptune's kingdom,
our realm.

Please, my child, do not grieve,
I am here.
You just cannot see me yet.

We will be able to gracefully follow
currents known only to the Ocean.
To swim joyfully over cities of coral,
adorn our hair and bodies with jewels,

lost to the upper world, eons ago, when
pirates plundered the seas at will;
then lost what they had plundered
When Neptune said, "These are MINE!"

Please, my child, do not grieve,
I am here,
You just cannot see me yet.

On the day you depart the landlocked world
I will be there to greet you.
To welcome with loving arms
and hold you with all the love withheld,
I love you. I just could not, off times, say it well;
As I had been taught in my own time –
"T will make her o'er proud!"

I am proud, I do love you.
I can hardly wait, though I would not deny you
the years you have left,
to take you to that place
where we, the Mermaids live.

Please my child, do not grieve.
I am here,
You just cannot see me yet.

But listen, I sing siren song for you!
Hear it?
In every ocean wave lapping gently on the shore,
in every beautiful, salt-laden wind.

In sea-bird's cry, in storm-tossed surf,
It is my voice calling.
Those are not just sounds by the shore
it is my voice, calling the only way I can, for now.

Please, my child, do not grieve.
I am here.
You just cannot see me yet.

Windsong and merbabes have brought me news;
Others of our kind have been born.
I will watch over them, each and every time they set baby
steps into our beautiful realm.
Give all of those to follow, love of the sea.
teach them all to swim, and to learn their special heritage.
For they are all one of us, yet to be!

Please, my child, do not grieve.
I am here.
You just cannot see me yet.

I now live where Mermaids live.
And cannot break the rules.
I will be waiting, arms held wide
to greet every woman of our kind.

Do not grieve.
I am here.
You just cannot see me yet.

We will be restored, to all our youth and beauty,

I will show you all of Ocean realm.
We will dance amid the ships anciently sunk
and filled with treasure.
We will adorn long hair, floating about us
to compass 'round slender waists
with priceless gold.
And adorn soft-skinned throats
with jewels, the envy of any Queen on Earth.

I await you my child,
and the children and grandchildren of my child;

We will enter Mermaid realm together
I will always guide you safely there.

Do not grieve my child,
I am here.
You just cannot see me yet.

But I do wonder, e'en now;
did we sacrifice our fins, did we live always in pain
for the love of a man?
Not many of them proved to be worthy.
I found my own, perfect love after many years
searching among lesser beings.
I wait him, with loving arms to heal him.
When it is his time to come home.
I have never loved another, half so well.

Please, my husband,
do not grieve.

I am here.
You just cannot hear me yet.

Oh, how I await the day.
Meet me when your spirit soars,
in that beloved place where you released me to the sea.
I will know, believe me.
The young ones will tell me –
"Your Merman returns to you!"

I will hurry there to the place we both so loved
and where you had to leave me –
Call you home to me, when your spirit too, tires.
Greet you again, as all your young male beauty returns.
In joyful reunion, we will be wed again.
Neptune our minister
all sea gods rejoicing.
All of sea realm gathering to welcome you,
Our honeymoon castle girded round about
with smiling dolphins and their babies,
guarding our privacy, so that we
can rejoice in love once more.

Do not fear death, oh thou whom I love,
we will meet again.
You just cannot hear me yet.

But, as darkness approaches,
Look toward the light.
I will be there, by my love's promise.
I have never forgotten you –

nor your loving care for those times when I was so ill.
Listen for my Siren song, it is me, beloved.
Do not fear, my love, my arms will enfold you
welcome you back
to the Ocean we loved so well.

Be not lonely my love.
I am here.
You just cannot hear me yet.

And we shall share bright sunny days,
Rest on still waters of the night
and play among St. Elmo's fire, our bodies lit with ghostly
green, then we, all rejoicing, will guard some more
calling, to those who still follow.

Do not grieve, our children.
We are here.
You just cannot hear us yet.

The Beats # 12

The beats rejecting progress found
other ways of perceiving the world.
Asian ideas expressed the
individual from within. We as
men didn't need to seek out
reality. We need to perceive ourselves
by our toys. It became an intuition
or imagination coming from the
unconscious which made us able to
understand the outside. Maybe people
were not trapped in their bodies
or on the earth. Perhaps to fully live and
to die at peace. All that is needed
is to be at peace with yourself. Why
would you need the permission of
anybody or anything of this earth?

Religions Everywhere

In the democratic times we
have about us, we can shake off
The leaves of religious authority.
Everybody wants their knowledge to
come from a single crop. It it's not
all in one place, man would rather
not put forth the effort to obtain it.
It's easy to see a single religion.
Harder to believe the world
contains many.

In the Midst of Things

All the losses of men are
from the disobedience
and the feelings of those
who have rebelled then fallen.
A leader has spoken of a
prophecy, the arrival of a new
creature. Chaos has shown
the way and the creatures have
a Savior an angel will volunteer
to die for the creatures. They can sing
the hymns in honor of their Leader.
The son of Light stepped forward, and with
his powers he battled those
who had fallen. With their
defeat they must return to the hisses of Hell.

Children's

There was a time in America
when a family comprised seven or
so children. Obvious financial and
health breakthroughs must have occurred.
Couples began to marry early, sex
was not then against any of societies
rules. Babies began to be born after
only seven or eight months. Unions began
to become faster. Religion came but
all a formality. Now only what
matters is what denomination a
man is.

Equal

No wager is as important as
the one which undertakes the
question. Does God exist? We all know
he is or he is not. For some there
never was a question. For others there
are nothing but questions. If neither
answer was correct and both held
the same number of properties.
It would be logical to believe in
a God. All things being equal.

Thought

With Capitalism there is no
time to deal with abstract thought.
Everyone and everything is always
in some type of motion. Some still
quest for money and power. But
striving for fortune does not help
bring about anything real.
It's too difficult to
stay on a single task with money
being whirled about men like
a current from an ocean,
pushed and pulled
back and forth. By a power greater
than themselves.

The Club

If a government feels the need
to be unjust to its people. Then it
should expect the people to be
unjust to it. Some times violence can
follow along. The black man, Indian,
Mexican, and the poor white man are
no more free than the days of slavery.
There is no honor when you carry no
hope. The government of this new world
order think their walls can not be
breached. But the bombs will deliver
and death will follow. The old clubs
of the rich will go away.

Silent Rain

All at once they came
No two quite the same
A magic we've all known
A beauty of their own.

They bring a certain peace
Though at times we wish they'd cease
Never making a single sound
As they gather around.

Sometimes they stay awhile
And to children bring a smile
Or simply disappear
Never knowing they were born.

Falling from the sky
Until they gently lie
Sparkling in the sun
Turning into none.

Silent rain, it came to me
Something you must see
For they never make a sound
Snowflakes floating to the ground.

Autumn

As leaves fall softly to the ground
the silence is broken from my feet
as they go through a path of bright yellow, reds and oranges
a rainbow of leaves

A shower of sunrays comes through a birch
warming my soul with contentment
a wren chirps to another
as a lonely butterfly flutters by

As I stop to breathe in the splendor of colors and silence
I realize how fortunate I am in this life and what I have
been given
slowly inhaling the beauty of this season
I remind myself of all the things I've taken for granted

As I walk along this wondrous beauty
I realize it will soon end
Newborn snowflakes will fall replacing these colors with a
virgin white
I turn around for one last look that become a memory

Soon it will be gone

Desert Dirt

I remember holes in my shoes
cardboard boxes, cut into foot shapes
carefully placed into each shoe
to stop from getting blisters
on the bottoms of my feet

Gravel, dirt and sand
from the desert dirt roads
always found a way to get in,
to rub on my heel
or my baby toe.

A blister would develop
the only way to make it not so uncomfortable
was to go to the sewing box,
burn the tip of the needle for sterilization
and poke a hole in the blister.

My feet were tough-skinned
Sometimes difficult to pop
but I felt joy and relief
watching the liquid ooze out
like blood from a cut.

Only then, would the blister not hurt
only then, could I put on
a bandage, my sock and shoe
and continue playing
in the gravel and sand
of the desert dirt.

A Happening

It happened.
I don't know why
and I don't know how
but it did.
Love blossomed
again
for the millionth time
in our
relationship.
Through our years
of life, laughter and tears
we come and go
emotionally.
Like
a wooden
roller coaster ride
getting dangerously close
to the edge
without falling.
Falling
into a deep
oblivion of feelings
ranging from
love
to nothingness
and back again.

Heart Carved

I still ponder on the stout tree,
where she carved a heart around
our initials.
It stood out proud as though it
were a first medal.
Our time, when we shared dreams,
rambled on for hours, held close,
and loved as only fairy tales
could comprehend.
Now the heart carved is just a wound
on an aging tree.

Regret

Welcome, pretty apparition
from out of nowhere
or dreary eyes that face reality..
Retribution for the past
Cannot amend inequity..
Still, you reach out
lend your warm hand
from long, long ago..

A Prayer for a Friend

Among the ivy and the roses
Where tears of loss are shed
By lovers now forgotten,
By the living for the dead.

The ghosts of sadness linger
In the mist of blinding haze,
In search of one another,
Through the fog of yesterdays.

May the angel of good fortune
Give you guidance from above.
May your days be filled with magic,
And your nights with perfect love.

May you find your kindred spirit;
May his heart be pure and true.
May your soul be resurrected,
And your life begin anew.

The Magic of the Music

She takes her place in time of need
Her fingers run up and down the keys
We listen and are lost from our space
Most the time you never see her face

The trumpets sound from the walls of Jericho
The waters call from Galilee and off we go
She leads us with such love and passion
Bring in her own flare and fashion

Never asking for even a thanks
No money for to take to the banks
Just a heart free of pain and warm inside
And a wondrous smile built from pride

If we don't take the times to give you grace
Remember that there is one of a higher place
He will always hold you close and dear
Because you have taken your time to help us hear

A Swingset

The swings are strong arms,
Cradled to make a seat.
The chains are another person,
Holding up the man who cradled his arms,
So the child can swing.

The rings are big hands,
Curved up for a good grip.
The chains are the rest of the body,
Holding the man upside-down,
So the child can swing.

The trapeze bar is two strong fingers,
Held pointing each other to form a bar.
The chains are the arms,
Holding the rest of the man upside-down,
So the child can swing.

The slide is a full-length man,
Tilting upward to form a slope.
The bars holding up the slide,
Are people standing tall,
So the child can slide.

The posts holding up the swingset,
Are strong bodies stacked up high.
The cross-bar across the top,
Is three men holding each other's ankles,
So the child can have all his fun.

Virginia City is Still Alive and Well

Back when Nevada was a brand new territory,
Her crown jewel Virginia City was in its full glory.
It was a lively, thriving place packed full of money and mirth
And is was known as one of the richest places on earth.
They came by the thousands from eastern states and the western seaports,
A smorgasbord of people of all types and sorts,
Treasure seekers poured in from all directions in a solid steady stream,
some down to their last dollar but still clinging to their dream.
Some industrious ones got wealthy buying shares of the Comstock lode,
while others made their fortunes from the V & T Railroad.
Most of the men drew wages hauling freight or working the ranches,
or doing shifts in the dangerous mines where they took their chances.
Virginia City was wild and wooly and the activity seldom ceased.
Saloon girls flashed their smiles as unsuspecting souls were fleeced.
The gambling hall owners were intent on taking every cent of the laborer's pay
and miners would lose in a very short time all the gold they'd found that day.
A place called Piper's Opera House was the social center of the town

And heroes and singing stars performed in this theatre of great renown.
It provided a cultural vein of sorts for the teamsters, cowboys and miners
who gladly parted their hard earned wages to see the famous headliners.
The City was a hub of financial commerce until about eighteen seventy-eight.
Then the gold and silver mines played out and left the town to its fate.
Just like how a well dries up and no more water is to be found,
Virginia City, who was always on top seemed to be on her way down.
With the loss of so much revenue the town folks knew the score
Because love goes out the window when poverty comes through the door.
Most of the affluent moved to San Francisco to spend their lion's share
and the miners moved on to rumored strikes to try their luck elsewhere.
But Virginia City is still alive and well today like it was back in that time.
And just as many people visit it now, as when it was in its prime.
It remains a point of historical interest and quite a tourist attraction.
Thanks to all the money they spend, it's still an old west town packed full of action

www.ingramcontent.com/pod-product-compliance
Lightning Source LLC
Chambersburg PA
CBHW021023090426
42738CB00007B/875